Joni Eareckson Tada

Secret STRENGTH JOURNAL

MULTNOMAH

Portland, Oregon 97266

Edited by Larry R. Libby
Design by Brenda Jose and Judy Quinn
Cover painting by Joni Eareckson Tada

SECRET STRENGTH
© 1988 by Joni, Inc.
Published by Multnomah Press
Portland, Oregon 97266

Multnomah Press is a ministry of Multnomah School of the Bible,
8435 Northeast Glisan Street, Portland, Oregon 97220

Printed in the United States of America

Library of Congress Cataloging-in-Publication Data

Tada, Joni Eareckson.
    Secret strength/Joni Eareckson Tada.
        p. cm.
    Includes index.
    ISBN 0-88070-238-9 : $14.95
    1. Meditations, I. Title.
BV4832.2T3 1988
248.4—dc19   88-12053
ISBN 0-88070-244-3 (journal)   CIP

88 89 90 91 92 93 94 95 – 8 7 6 5 4 3 2 1

Contents

PART 1

Secrets of His Strength

PART 2

Secrets of His Character

PART 3

Secrets of His Grace

PART 4

Secrets of Praise

Dear Friends. . .

If you're like me, many of the thoughts, insights, and impressions the Lord shows you in His Word or through His people tend to slip through your fingers if you don't take time to get them down on paper. Some of those thoughts hit me—clear and strong—in the middle of the night, and since I can't jump out of bed and write them down, I have to carefully memorize them until I have the opportunity to "borrow" someone's hands the next morning.

But most of you don't have *that* problem. All you need are the encouragement and discipline to open your Bible, sharpen your pencil, and put some of those choice thoughts and discoveries into writing.

I hope and pray that SECRET STRENGTH will nudge you into a closer walk with our heavenly Father. The "Stronghold" applications at the end of each reading were intended to help you personalize the daily readings and take that all-important "next step" . . . from good intentions to positive actions! The journal you hold in your hands simply repeats those questions and suggestions, and gives you room to record your personal responses.

This is neither "Joni's journal" nor "Joni's journey." The spiritual adventure which lies ahead belongs to you . . . and Him. It is to *you* God longs to reveal His secrets. It is in *you* God desires to display His strength. Please know that my earnest prayers are with you as you set your heart to know Him.

PART 1

Secrets of His Strength

Read 1 Corinthians 2:1-5. Can you imagine the apostle Paul weak and fearful—even trembling? Why do you think he thought of himself that way? How does his example speak to you? Take heart knowing that if God did such great things through a man who often trembled in weakness and fear, He can surely use you!

_____

"He's really _____ to that pole in the storm!" If you were a news reporter describing the man in the yellow slicker, what verbs would come to mind? Clinging? Grabbing? Clutching?

Now, what verbs would you use to describe how *you* have held on to God when you were hit hard with storms?

The next time you see a storm brewing in your life, hang on to this "telephone pole"—Deuteronomy 4:29-31.

Complaints, murmurings, and grumbling. That's how the Israelites are remembered for their lack of contentment. For a closer look, start at Exodus 16:3-5. Manna from heaven wasn't enough, was it?

Now flip to Numbers 11:4-10. Would you like to know how the Lord finally satisfied their desires? Read aloud—and laugh aloud—through verses 18-20.

Project: Compile your wants and God's wants. How many of them match?

Prayer: Help me, Father, to subtract my desires . . . to not be picky, to not always insist on having things exactly my own way. Forgive me if I keep adding more and more wants, for You know just what I need. And in that I am content.

"Will you obey?" That's a good question. The verse in our reading, 1 Corinthians 10:13, is good. But go a step further and start reading from the very first verse in chapter 10. How are the examples of Moses and his followers a warning to you?

If you have ever said, "Oh, I would never behave like that," type out verse 12 on a card, stick it on your bathroom mirror, and memorize it for your own good.

_____

_____

_____

_____

_____

_____

_____

_____

_____

_____

_____

_____

_____

_____

_____

_____

_____

_____

_____

_____

Let's keep the lines of communication open today between us, Christ's body, and Jesus, our Head. To test those open lines, begin with Matthew 6:6-13. What inspires—or convicts—you most about this Scripture? Is your communication with God two-way?

The lines *are* open, so make sure you use them this week.

_____

_____

_____

_____

_____

_____

_____

_____

_____

_____

_____

_____

_____

_____

_____

_____

_____

_____

_____

_____

_____

_____

What makes the difference between the wax and the clay? If the Holy Spirit has got your heart even slightly ready, then you can be the wax that melts, too. I hope you will see yourself as that wax today, ready to be molded and melted into Jesus' image. Don't bother that you've been responding to the small irritations as some chunk of old, dry, hardened clay. As you go about the rest of *this* day, facing those everyday pressures, let the Son do His work. The wax will melt, and you'll be all the better for it. Read 1 Peter 4:12-19, 5:6-11.

Sometimes we feel more secure if we can present a clean, starched impression of our Christian walk. But look at what Paul says in 1 Corinthians 1:26-29. The fellowship of Christ includes even the people whom some consider "embarrassing blotches." How can you see yourself in this portion of Scripture? Think of how you might reach out to those believers you know are in pain or are embarrassed by failure. Find some practical ways to encourage them. Help them see that their example could be a convincing and convicting testimony to unbelievers.

If you're hurting right now, hold on to the thoughts expressed in 2 Corinthians 4:11-18. What reasons does Paul offer for not losing heart in our daily struggles? Look closer at verses 16-18. What is Paul's counsel? As you close this book, take a few moments to "fix your eyes" on the Lord Jesus.

Ask yourself—do you long to know Christ? Or do you only know *about* Him. Take a look at Philippians 3:7-11. When Paul says he wants to know Christ in verse 10, what does his desire also include? How about it . . . would you like to join the fellowship of sharing Christ's suffering? How can you be "like Him in His death"?

When it seems problems are about to break on top of you, don't bury your head in the sand . . . face them with courage and confidence. What will help you stand your ground? Look at the first three sentences in James 4:7-8. Underline the verb of action in each sentence and make a commitment today to face your problems with that advice in mind.

Dig into a jewelry box, find a cross which hasn't been worn in a while and hang it where you'll be able to see it often. Let it be a reminder, for a while, of the high price Christ paid on His cross for you.

The horrible realities of the crucifixion tend to become obscured with the passage of time. Perhaps now would be an appropriate time to refresh your memory about the sacrifice your Lord offered on your behalf.

Carve out some time today so that you can spend several quiet and secluded moments with Matthew 27:27-50.

The question bears repeating: Were you going to help someone this past week but then politely, reservedly stayed at arm's length? How about that card of encouragement . . . did you ever send it? Stop right now and put your letter-writing paper and telephone book in clear view as a reminder to carry through before the day is done. Memorize 2 Corinthians 1:3-4.

_____

Make time this week to read the book of Ruth (don't worry, it's only four chapters long!). Get an inside look at the way friends and relatives should care for one another. Notice the way Ruth, Naomi, and Boaz supported each other in a godly way.

Is there someone in your family you've been caring for? For whose notice and praise have you been laboring? Do you want to impress your relative and those who notice? Or do you perform your tasks as a service of praise to God? Learn from Ruth those principles of higher service.

Read Isaiah 25:4-5. Think of the last time you enjoyed a picnic at the park or a party in your back yard on a summer day. Describe the relief you felt sitting in the shade, thinking of at least three ways you were comforted. Have you felt the same kind of comfort resting in the shadow of God's presence?

How would you describe the difference between "passive" and "active" waiting. Read Hosea 12:6. What does this verse advise us to do while we wait? How long must we wait on God? Get into the habit of actively waiting, and before you know it you'll feel those eagle wings underneath you!

_____

_____

_____

_____

_____

_____

_____

_____

_____

_____

_____

_____

_____

_____

_____

_____

_____

_____

_____

_____

_____

_____

If you were to lead an army against the Midianites, Amalekites, and a host of hostile foreigners, how many people would you want on your team? Would thirty-two thousand trained soldiers be enough? Gideon thought so, but the Lord had other ideas. For a good story on how God delights to use weak people (and weakened armies!) read Judges chapter 7.

When you look at today's responsibilities, do you feel God expects too much of you? If so, read Ephesians 3:16-19 for strength and encouragement.

_____

_____

_____

_____

_____

_____

_____

_____

_____

_____

_____

_____

_____

_____

_____

_____

_____

_____

_____

_____

_____

_____

_____

_____

_____

The writer of the book of Hebrews also thought of God as a shelter. Take a look at Hebrews 13:4-6. Notice that he even quotes Psalm 118:6, adding this wonderful thought: "He Himself has said, 'I will never desert you, nor will I ever forsake you.'"

Our friend in Hebrews is describing exactly what we have been thinking about for the last couple of pages: Our Lord is a *shelter* for His much-loved sons and daughters. But He makes these statements in the context of a discussion on (1) Sex and marriage, and (2) money (verses 4-5). Take some time to read through these few verses, considering how the Lord's beautiful offer of refuge, help, and security apply to these two crucial areas of our lives.

If you're going through a winter time in your soul, read Romans chapter 6 today. To gain extra insight, read it once in your regular Bible, and again in a paraphrase of the Scriptures such as *The Living Bible*. Let the promise of "newness of life" in verse 4 remind you that spring can begin *today* in your heart.

STRONGHOLD

The dictionary says that *noble* means, "Grand, splendid, magnificent; having greatness of character and excellent qualities." Wouldn't you like to be one of God's chosen vessels for *noble* use? You can be, you know. Read again 2 Timothy 2:21, paying special attention to the last part of the verse. What kind of work could be considered noble? How can you prepare yourself to be used for noble purposes?

49

Do you use a favorite toothbrush that's worn and thin? Or an old comb with missing teeth? Or a dog-eared address book filled with marks and scribbles? Or a spatula that's been flipping pancakes for twenty years? Or an antiquated Underwood manual typewriter? Or an ancient Boy Scout jackknife with a stiff blade? In your hands, these trusted items perform best. You prefer them. You choose them.

Let one of these simple, everyday items be a reminder to you of how God wants to use you and your strengths and weaknesses. Why do you think God has chosen you for the special tasks He's given you? Why do you think He prefers to use you for the ministry He has in mind for your family? Your co-workers? Your neighbors?

Have you ever stopped to ask a person for directions? He or she tells you to go three blocks north, left at the signal, stay to the right, and go two stop signs to the next intersection—and you're more confused than ever. You wish that person would say, "Follow me. I'm headed in that direction."

Jesus said virtually the same thing in John 14:5-6. Did Jesus say He was only one way among many ways? Or is He the only way? Thank your Lord right now that He does not hand you an impossible creed as a road map for life. He offers you Himself!

Someone has said, "Sow a thought, reap an action . . . sow an action, reap a habit . . . sow a habit, reap a character." Drifting from God starts in small ways with little thoughts. To keep the current of your thoughts in line, find a King James Bible and look up 2 Corinthians 10:5. Can your thoughts be controlled? Who gives you the power to do so?

We often depend on our own skills and abilities when life seems easy, but we only turn to God when we've exhausted other resources. Dependence is not defeat. Dependence is glorious. Read what David, a powerful warrior and king, wrote on the subject in Psalm 62, especially verses 7-8.

Rely...lean...trust...depend...count on...bank on... pin your faith on God. Will you let your problems and pressures today drive you to Him? Rely on God—first!

_____

_____

_____

_____

_____

_____

_____

_____

_____

_____

_____

_____

_____

_____

_____

_____

_____

_____

_____

_____

_____

_____

Lamentations chapter 3 is full of "lifeline" verses, rich with hope, encouragement, and inspiration. Why not investigate them for yourself?

For a little background, Lamentations was the "book of lamenting" that Jeremiah wrote during the crisis of the Babylonian invasion. Tough times they were. Look at verses 22 through 24. How about verse 33 for encouagement? And don't forget verse 40 for a real lifesaver.

Facing tough times today? Grab hold of these lifeline verses.

When it comes to discerning spiritual truth, we are all mentally handicapped apart from the teaching and guidance of the Spirit of God. With this in mind, read John 14:16-17. Will the Holy Spirit ever leave you? Now look at verses 25-27. Exactly what will the Spirit teach you? Take a few moments and thank God for the ministry of His Holy Spirit, a powerful Person who is on your side, working through, for, and with you.

"Open my eyes that I may see, visions of truth Thou hast for me . . ." I like that old familiar hymn. Oh, that we would be like the two blind men who, when asked by Christ what they wanted, simply replied, "Lord, that our eyes may be opened." Are your eyes open to spiritual reality today . . . or do you feel overwhelmed by the forces that seem arrayed against you? Read Ephesians 1:15-23. What sorts of things should you be able to see when God gives you the "eyes of the heart" described in verse 18?

PART 2

Secrets of His Character

Paul was a good one for greeting trials with a joyful mindset. Just take a look at Philippians 1:12-18. Even though Paul was writing from prison, his letter is full of joy. In fact, the words *joy* or *rejoice* are used fourteen times in Philippians.

How can you, like Paul, welcome your trials as friends? Try greeting them with God's Word. Take time to memorize Philippians 4:4 and make it your "verse of welcome" when your next trial sneaks up on you.

STRONGHOLD

Flip to the end of Matthew's gospel and marvel at the very last verse. Jesus' closing words are the capstone of His entire ministry—and what comforting words they are. The Lord went through heaven and hell to assure you with this last and great statement He made on earth. Let His goodness right now crumble any resistance, any doubt or stubbornness in your heart. Allow His goodness to lead you into a prayer of repentance.

Love, as it says in the last verse before 1 Corinthians 13, is "the most excellent way" to reach out to someone who's hurting. Why not take this chance to read 1 Corinthians 13 and think of a hurting friend who needs His supernatural love.

I can show *patience* toward my friend who suffers by
_____ .

It would be a *very kind* thing if I would _____ .

Do I *envy* others who seem better able to help? Forgive me, Lord.

Love is not *proud* or *boastful*. Am I that way when I offer a hand? Let me only be proud in You, Lord.

I can avoid being *rude* or *insensitive* by _____ .

Why am I helping? What is my motive? Am I *self-seeking*?

If my hurting friend rejects my offers to help, Lord, keep me from becoming *easily angered* or *keeping a record of wrongs*.

How can I help my friend *rejoice in the truth*?

I can *protect* my friend by _____ .

I will *trust* God to bless my efforts to help.

I will *hope* for my friend when he or she feels hopeless.

I will *persevere* even though I don't see immediate results.

_____

_____

_____

_____

_____

_____

Read Revelation 21 to help you throw open the shutters of heaven today. Consider verse 21: If the streets of heaven are paved with gold, then it stands to reason that in heaven gold won't have a great deal of value. It's primary use will be paving material for streets! If gold and precious gems won't hold value in heaven, what things will? How can you lay up the kind of treasure which will last for eternity?

_____

Pick an attribute of God—wisdom, mercy, purity, tenderness, justice, or some other character quality of your Lord. Meditate for a few moments on how marvelously God reveals Himself through that attribute.

In your prayers during the rest of the day—whether for your family or friends, for emergencies or even for incidentals—link all of your requests to that special attribute of your heavenly Father. Not only will your prayers have power, but you will get to know God more intimately.

Let me ask you a question straight out.

Do you occasionally find yourself grasping for the future as though the present didn't quite satisfy? Do you sometimes feel you miss the best of life while looking the other way, preoccupied with shaping your future? Look up Psalm 39:4 and make it your prayer today.

As Francis Schaeffer said, "Made in God's image, man was made to be great, he was made to be beautiful, and he was made to be creative in life and art . . ."

Just think! You are a work of art—a painting, poem, symphony, or ballet. Just as the potter will shape and mold a piece of clay into a beautiful vase, God touches your life with His creative genius. Read about it in Jeremiah 18:1-6, and rejoice that He has chosen the perfect design, the best composition just for you!

_____

_____

_____

_____

_____

_____

_____

_____

_____

_____

_____

_____

_____

_____

_____

_____

_____

_____

Read Habakkuk 3. The prophet Habakkuk was shaken to the soul by a God-given glimpse into the future. Israel's existence hung by the thinnest of threads. A cruel and powerful army would sweep in from the north and destroy everything Habakkuk held dear. In his perplexity and sorrow, the prophet bowed before the sovereignty of God, finally yielding the full weight of his worry. His song of trust in Habakkuk 3:16-19 is one of the most beautiful in all of Scripture. Follow this godly man's lead today as you release your fears . . . and rejoice in God's sovereign control.

Read John 3:16-21. Why do some people refuse to "see the Light"? Think of several unbelievers on your prayer list. Is it possible they may feel threatened by your desire to obey God and do what is right? Perhaps they're afraid the light in you may expose some darkness in their lives. Don't let that discourage you. Keep praying they will come to see how much better it is to live in light rather than darkness. In fact . . . why not pray for them right now?

Take a few moments to read Mark 14:3-7.

The woman in Bethany did a very extravagant and, in the eyes of some, wasteful thing. Praise is like that. There are *so* many things to pray about, so many needs—the poor, the homeless, the aged, not to mention family and financial problems. If time is short, shouldn't it mostly be spent on praying over these needs?

But Jesus reminds us in Mark 14 that praise—extravagant, lavish, and profuse—comes before any request. There is nothing wasteful about loving praise. Take some moments right now and offer up a "sacrifice of praise" to the One who sacrificed so much for you.

Let me guess. You've put it off long enough. Over and over you've been reminded by the Spirit to make a home in your heart for God's Word. And today's reading has only reinforced it. Isn't now as good a time as any to once-and-for-all do something about it?

"But where do I begin?" you might ask. One of the best plans I know of is the *Topical Memory System* published by the Navigators. I've used it and the plan has definitely helped (they're not paying me to say this, either). Why not check it out at your local Christian bookstore?

It's exciting to think that as we are found faithful in our little corner of His kingdom, God will begin to slowly extend and expand our love for Him and for others.

Read Matthew 25:14-28 and be joyful about the day God will say to *you*, "Well done, good and faithful servant! You have been faithful with a few things; I will put you in charge of many things. Come and share your Master's happiness!"

But wait a minute. Are you afraid of your little corner expanding and extending? Sound like too much responsibility? Take a closer look at Matthew 25:15, breathe a sigh of relief, and finish off with these questions.

1. The Master divided the money among His servants according to their _____ . No one received more or less money than he could handle.

2. Money, as used in Matthew 25, represents any kind of resource we are given. God gives me _____, and _____, and _____. Am I using well what God has given me?

3. The issue is not how _____ we have, but what we _____ with what we have.

A verse such as John 3:16 is probably old and very familiar territory to you. You may even know it by heart—"For God so loved the world that He gave His only begotten Son . . ."

You've probably read it ten thousand times, but it can still remain fresh for you. How? First, ask the Holy Spirit to help you. Then, read the verse slowly several times, each time placing special emphasis and thoughtful meditation on one word. "For GOD so loved the world . . . For God SO loved the world . . . For God so LOVED the world" . . . and so on.

Prayerfully approach other favorite verses this way and begin to understand God's ideas for you—fresh and new!

The early church had problems being unified, too. Paul exposes the problem in 1 Corinthians 1:10-13. Read it for an eye-opening account of just how destructive it can be when the parts of Christ's church start vying for attention. What advice does Paul give these warring factions? Continue on to 1 Corinthians 3 for the inside story.

Ask yourself: Do I secretly think I'm better than other Christians? How can I better cooperate today with someone I've been competing against? Do I want Jesus to be the focus of my life? Of my fellowship?

Take a look at Romans 11:22 and notice the two characteristics of God. Do you see a balance? Kindness is one characteristic of God. Sternness might be considered its complement. Match a characteristic of God listed on the left with one on the right. Remember, there's no room for a one-sided view of our Lord.

Power	Tenderness
Anger	Approachability
Justice	Forgiveness
Wrath	Meekness
Strength	Mercy
Unapproachability	Gentleness

_____

_____

_____

_____

_____

_____

_____

_____

_____

_____

_____

_____

_____

_____

_____

_____

Who is it who feels he has done God a favor by obeying Him? He is described in Isaiah 29:13.

But who is it who obeys God out of humility and sincere submission? Psalm 15 provides a clear snapshot.

Now the question: Which best describes *you*? Make it your prayer today to obey out of humility and submission.

Promises . . . they get broken, forgotten, or ignored. It's unfortunate, but often people don't come through on their promises.

John 16:33 offers a twofold promise. "In this world you will have trouble. But take heart! I have overcome the world." Why is it we can take heart despite our troubles? You guessed it—because Jesus has overcome. How does Jesus help you to overcome?

_____

_____

_____

Take heart. Jesus is a promise-keeper!

_____

_____

_____

_____

_____

_____

_____

_____

_____

_____

_____

_____

_____

_____

People have painted pictures of the Lord Jesus throughout the centuries. But these capture only a frozen image, a stiff and motionless representation. God wants us to be "living pictures" of Him. Read 1 John 4:7-12 and think of ways you can color other peoples' impressions of God. Say to yourself: "What I do and say will give people a clearer impression of Jesus than any painting ever could!"

It's easy to pray with compassion and empathy for those we love or respect. It's harder to pray for people in trouble—a neighbor with AIDS, a church member who's schizophrenic, or a homosexual struggling to change his lifestyle.

Take five minutes right now to pray for an individual who comes to mind. Still fighting spiritual snobbery? Try using Colossians 1:9-14 as a prayer guideline for that person, paying special attention to all the good things you're praying for him.

Read 2 Samuel 11 to get an inside look at the way David kept trying to sweep his sin under the carpet. One thing piled on top of another until Nathan confronts him in the next chapter. Finally, David breaks. His heartbroken confession is recorded in Psalm 51.

What "little sins" in David's life might have led to his great fall? What "little sins" frequently go unconfessed and unrepented in your life? Stop and put your finger on them now. Sweep them out from under the carpet of your conscience and present them in confession before God.

_____

_____

_____

_____

_____

_____

_____

_____

_____

_____

_____

_____

_____

_____

_____

_____

Don't we have a great God? Just take a look at Acts 17:24-28. If the person being described were anyone other than God, you might think he was on an ego trip. But God's ego trip has a very special purpose. Locate God's purpose in this section of Scripture and make it your personal prayer today.

I knew a disabled person who once said, "I used to have a million questions and no answers. I still don't have the answers. But you know what? I don't have the questions, either."

Come up with one question for God you've been putting on the back burner. Now read Romans 8:38-39. Commit yourself to read and meditate on those two verses every day for the next week.

_____

_____

_____

_____

_____

_____

_____

_____

_____

_____

_____

_____

_____

_____

_____

_____

_____

As you read Psalm 121, personalize it by inserting your own name in each verse, just to see how personally God involves Himself with your life's details.

_____

Think of all the different kinds of mirrors you have around your house—everything from the large beveled mirror in your living room to your little, round, compact mirror. Mirrors may come in different sizes and shapes, but they all do the same thing—reflect!

Now take a closer look at 2 Corinthians 3:18. Have you ever considered that you are a mirror which reflects the glory of the Lord? No matter how big or small you see yourself in God's family, God wants you to reflect His Son's image.

People usually see the Lord glorified in my life when I am able to _____.

STRONGHOLD

Have you ever borrowed a tool from a neighbor and had it break in your hand? A small inconvenience to most, but quite a big concern for you! Does God care about such little annoyances? Just in case you doubt, read 2 Kings 6:1-7.

Has God taken you into His confidence lately? Has he revealed some special truth to you? Something about His love that before seemed incomprehensible, or His plans that formerly seemed an enigma? If so, take a moment to praise God for choosing to be intimate with you.

If you haven't heard any good secrets lately, remember this: "Blessed is the man who always fears the Lord . . ." When you fear the Lord, it's like cupping your ear so you may hear Him!

_____

Open your Bible to 2 Corinthians 8:9. I challenge you to spend at least five minutes today pondering what the Lord Jesus gave up to become your Savior. Let your thoughts and meditation bring you to your knees in adoration of this great God who humbled Himself . . . for you.

PART 3

Secrets of His Grace

How does your big Brother, the Lord Jesus, feel about naming you as one of the family? Flip to Hebrews 2:5-15 and take a little pride in the way Jesus speaks of His relationship to you.

Verse 11 affirms that the Son of God is "not ashamed" to call us His brothers and sisters. What reasons does the passage give for our Brother's decision to "share in our humanity"? Think on that . . . and take some time before you get into bed tonight to tell Him what that decision means to you.

You've sung it scores of times in church, but have you put it to memory? And remember to sing it through the day when the worries of next week tempt you.

> *Great is Thy faithfulness! Great is Thy*
> *faithfulness!*
> *Morning by morning new mercies I see;*
> *All I have needed Thy hand hath provided;*
> *Great is Thy faithfulness, Lord, unto me!* [5]

With the idea that grace is the desire and power to do God's will, look more closely at Philippians 2:12-13. What do we call that work of God in our life? You guessed it—*grace*.

Read John 7:37-39. Can you grab the meaning of those powerful words in the context of the climate in which these people lived? The abundance or lack of water was a life-or-death issue. Why do you think Jesus used the analogy of a *river* instead of a "lake" or "pool" or some other body of water? What does that imply about the nature and quality of the life He offers to those who place their trust in Him?

_____

For a closer look at how Jesus handled self-pity in the life of one of His disciples, read John 21:20-23. Why was Peter so jealous of John? How did this magnify his own self-pity? Most importantly, what was Christ's response?

Make this your prayer:

Father, when I compare myself to others it only magnifies my misery. I've even doubted Your good plan for my life when I've been in tough times. Help me to listen when I hear You say, "What is that to You? You follow Me!" And most of all, help me to follow.

To dine at the King's table is a special privilege. God even has a banquet prepared—for His Son, the King, and for us. Read about it in Revelation 19:6-10 and rejoice that you're on the invitation list!

Here's an additional thought. If God filters trials and disappointments through His fingers, and we are those fingers, it gives us some real responsibililty toward one another. If suffering and discouragement are besieging your life, what can I do—as the very fingers of Jesus Christ—to protect you, to push away the harm, to wipe away your tears, to hold your hand or clasp your shoulder? To whom can you be the fingers of the Lord Jesus today?

Are you aware of a hurt today that could be healed if only you would take the initiative? What does Matthew 5:23-24 indicate about the practice of waiting for the other person to "come around"?

_____

_____

_____

_____

_____

_____

_____

_____

_____

_____

_____

_____

_____

_____

_____

_____

_____

_____

_____

_____

_____

_____

_____

_____

Do something small today. Listen in on a conversation between two grade schoolers. Read a chapter from *Little House on the Prairie*. Wind up a music box and hum along with the tune. Delight yourself in little, seemingly insignificant things.

And in case you think you're above such things, read the account in Matthew 19:13-14 of Jesus, the great Creator of the universe, enjoying time and small-talk with children. Was anyone too small in His eyes?

God is pleased to have your name included in His Son's family tree. In fact, look at 1 Corinthians 1:21. What exactly is God's attitude when it comes to your salvation? Why is He pleased to have you join His family?

Do a little investigation on your own family tree. How many relatives do you have who you hardly ever see? They may not know it, but they need prayer . . . your prayers. Why not list in your mind names of distant or close relatives and bring them before God in prayer today? Who knows? Through your prayers, some of them may one day end up on a limb of the family tree of Jesus as well!

Jesus talks a lot about cleansing and washing during His ministry on earth. In fact, washing His disciple's feet was the last act of service He performed before He went to the cross. Read about it in John 13:1-17. Notice our Lord's words in verses 14-17. How can you "wash the feet" of a friend or family member? How can you refresh and invigorate them? What should your attitude be?

Read Romans 5:1-5 and ask yourself this: What wonderful benefit grows out of "proven character"? As you come before your Lord in prayer today, ask Him to help you keep the perspective of these verses as pressures and problems enter your life in the coming week.

There is One who can enter your pain. The solitary Man, a man of sorrows who was acquainted with grief. Keep a bookmark in this page so you can refer to William Bathurst's fitting poem when pain knocks on your door in the coming days.

Lord Jesus, King of Pain,
Thy subject I;
Thy right it is to reign:
Oh, hear my cry,
And bid in me all longings cease
Save for Thy holy will's increase.

Thy right it is to reign
O'er all Thine own;
Then, if Thy love send pain,
Find there Thy throne,
And help me bear it unto Thee,
Who didst bear death and hell for me.

Lord Jesus, King of pain,
My heart's Adored,
Teach me eternal gain
Is Love's reward:
In Thee I hide me; hold me still
Till pain work all Thy perfect will.

_____

_____

_____

_____

_____

_____

_____

_____

Don't you love the clean-clear-through feeling of being able to look someone straight in the eyes? You don't feel insecure or fearful. You only feel the transparency of sheer confidence. Joy flows, not only from your heart, but toward the heart of your friend.

It's no different when looking into the face of God as we pray. Eye-to-eye contact is still the best test of confidence and transparency in any relationship.

Try looking up these three "face" verses—Psalm 27:8-9, Psalm 31:16, and Psalm 67:1—and then top it off with that joyful reminder in 1 John 3:2-3. One day we shall see Him face to face!

How clean-clear-through do you feel as you pray to God today?

Families are complex, their relationships intricate and involved. Some members fall apart in a crisis, others rise to the occasion and take charge.

It can be fascinating to take a close look at the way family members relate to each other. Take sisters, for instance—the way they talk together, the way they deal with problems, the way they laugh, cry, or get angry with each other.

For an inside look into Mary and Martha, find time today to read John 11:17-44. Notice how differently these sisters face the death of their brother . . . and the delay of their Lord. Which sister seems stronger? Who seems to take charge? Who is noted as crying?

Picture yourself at the scene—perhaps as a member of the family. How do you see yourself responding?

Just think—in Christ you are a brand new person on the inside. You're not simply a rehabilitated, shaped-up version with a couple of Band-Aids stuck on to cover the old self. You haven't merely turned over a new leaf. You are a new creation, living in vital union with Christ.

Turn to Romans 6:11. What does it mean to reckon, or consider, or count yourself dead to sin but alive to God? For a deeper look at these thoughts, read Romans 6 all the way through. Colossians 2:9-13 offers some exciting insight as well.

Contrasts. A black night seems to make the moon brighter. Purple irises brighten yellow daffodils and a dark gray Kansas sky makes the wheat look truly golden.

The Bible talks about contrasts in 2 Corinthians 4:7-12. Ponder Paul's words and then consider this: The supremely valuable message of salvation has been entrusted by God to you, a frail and fallible human being. You are holding this precious treasure in your body, a weak and perishable container. How does your life contrast—that is, show up best—the light and power of Christ within you?

"We can perhaps understand a God who would forgive sinners who crawl to Him for mercy," says Ken Taylor, "but a God who searches for sinners and then forgives them must have extraordinary love!"

This is the kind of love that prompted Jesus to come to earth to search for lost people and save them. This is the kind of extraordinary love God has for you. If your prayer life has been a trap of "mind games," if you feel far from God, don't despair. Take comfort by reading Luke 15:3-10. God is searching for you!

When King George II attended the London premiere of Handel's *Messiah*, it is said he was so touched by the "Hallelujah Chorus" that he rose and remained standing until its end. Of course, when the king stood up, the rest of the audience did, too. Since that time virtually all audiences have done the same.

Handel said that while composing the chorus, "I did think I did see all Heaven before me, and the great God Himself." It is one of the most glorious of all musical moments!

God, like a great composer, has you in mind as He composes the entire score of His kingdom. You are in His thoughts as He blends the parts into one great symphony. Want to hear what it's going to sound like? Turn to Revelation 5:11-14 and imagine yourself joining in the chorus of millions of angels.

Now, how about putting Handel's *Messiah* on the stereo and singing along? It's a great way to praise God!

CHAPTER 9

It breaks my heart to think of those unsympathetic disciples in Matthew 20 turning a deaf ear to Jesus at His deepest point of need. If I had been there, I would like to think I would have held my Lord's hand, looked straight into His eyes, and said, "Please . . . tell me all about it." That's what friends are for.

But do I—do you—*really* treat the Lord as a treasured friend?

Think of all the special things friends share—heart-to-heart talks, the sacrifice of time, wants and needs, joys and sorrows, love and companionship. Jesus covers His side of friendship with you in John 15:15. As you read those words, and then read through that whole chapter, ask yourself, *How can I be a better friend to Jesus?*

If you want an idea of how the Lord takes on His fair share of your load, read Matthew 11:28-30. Jesus had in mind a double-yoke, two oxen sharing the weight of the same burden. It was also the practice to put a younger ox in a yoke with an older, stronger, more experienced ox.

As you "plow" through a heavy, frustrating schedule yoked with Jesus Christ, which one of you will take most of the weight? From where does the "rest" come?

_____

As you read this, you may find yourself unsure of whether or not you're "lit." Perhaps you're uncertain you are truly a child of God.

Put to rest your doubts, once and for all. Quietly ask God to forgive you of all your sins. Accept the fact that the Lord Jesus Christ personally paid the penalty for your sins on His cross. Now ask Him to not only be your Savior, but Lord as well, believing He will give you His powerful Spirit to help you trust and obey Him.

Now, take out one of your dinner candles and light it.

Do you have the assurance that you are "lit," and not simply "enlightened"? Take a look at 2 Peter 1:5-11 and rejoice in the fact that you will one day receive a rich welcome into the eternal kingdom!

Do you feel confused, even betrayed by some sad series of circumstances in your life? Each of the following verses is like a spoonful of strong-tasting medicine, yet can be a healing influence in your life today. At first glance, the three verses will seem hard to fathom, but allow God to minister each as a dose, a healing balm to help soothe away the confusion and sense of betrayal.

"Blessed is the man whom God corrects; so do not despise the discipline of the Almighty" (Job 5:17, NIV).

"Come, let us return to the LORD. He has torn us to pieces but He will heal us; he has injured us but he will bind up our wounds" (Hosea 6:1, NIV).

"It was good for me to be afflicted so that I might learn your decrees" (Psalm 119:71, NIV).

The dictionary will tell you that to show mercy is to "refrain from harming or punishing an enemy . . . or to show kindness in excess of what may be expected . . . or to give compassionate treatment or relief of suffering."

For another story of God's mercy toward those who need it most, read Matthew 9:9-13 and ask yourself these questions:

1. What did our Lord mean when He said He came to help the sick and not the healthy?
2. How has God shown unexpected kindness to me this week?
3. How can I show mercy to one of my "enemies" today? Or compassion to one who is hurting?

_____

Learn some more secrets about grace!
Locate Ephesians 2:8-9 and learn that grace is a _____ of God.

Read Titus 2:11. Who is grace for? _____

Second Peter 3:18 says you can _____ in grace.

What does God require of us in 1 Peter 5:5 in order to receive grace? _____

There's one drawback, and it's listed in Hebrews 12:15. Grace can be _____.

_____ ❦ _____

_____

_____

_____

_____

_____

_____

_____

_____

_____

_____

_____

_____

_____

_____

_____

_____

_____

Take a look at the word *poison* in the dictionary and it will tell you it's a substance which, even if taken in small quantities, can cause illness or death.

Do we have even the vaguest notion of how our disobedience acts like poison—not only in our own lives but the lives of others? Hebrews 12:15 reads like a doctor's diagnosis and prescription: "Be careful that none of you fails to respond to the grace of God, for if he does there can spring up in him a bitter spirit which can poison the lives of many others" (Phillips).

Do a little self-diagnosis. What poison is there in your life for which the antidote of God's grace can be applied?

In prayer, ask God to apply His healing balm, His love and grace.

Is there anything you honestly lack? Are you convinced God truly supplies all of your needs? Are you sold on the fact that you are complete in Him?

If there's a shade of doubt, turn to Psalm 23 and zero in on the very first verse. You've read it scores of times before, but it will help you to read it one more time today.

Think of at least five ways of saying, "The Lord is my shepherd, I shall lack nothing."

_____

_____

_____

_____

_____

_____

_____

_____

_____

_____

_____

_____

_____

_____

_____

_____

_____

_____

_____

Jesus set us an example to follow in 1 Peter 2:23. So how do we follow an example like that? The advice is short and to the point in 1 Peter 3:8-9.

What do you think it means to "step on God's heels"? To get your imagination going, read Proverbs 3:5-6.

Did you catch that phrase, "In all your ways acknowledge Him . . ."? To "acknowledge" God is to step on His heels! If you want to follow God that closely it might mean

> . . . being *instant* in obedience
> . . . being *absolute* in your trust
> . . . praying *immediately* over a concern, or
> . . . responding *quickly* to a suggestion from the Holy Spirit.

Can you think of more ways you might "step on God's heels"? As you encounter twists and turns in your path today, acknowledge Him. And don't forget His promise . . . "He will make your paths straight."

Read Psalm 90 and gain a bit of the perspective that
Moses had on life. In view of the brevity of life, what
was Moses' prayer in verse 12? Carry that verse on a
file card today and take time to ponder its meaning.
Ask the Lord to grant you His perspective on time
and life as you seek to make the most of today's oppor-
tunities.

_____

_____

_____

_____

_____

_____

_____

_____

_____

_____

_____

_____

_____

_____

_____

_____

_____

_____

_____

_____

_____

_____

For those who belong to the heavenly Father, scientific demonstrations can refresh a sense of awe and wonder within us. These are not simply "patterns of nature," they are the designs of a master Designer! Read Job 28:20-28. What does Job say about wisdom in the creation around us? What is the essence of wisdom? Write Job 28:28 on a three-by-five card and read it several times today.

Read Hebrews 4:16. Let's dissect the verse, asking the standard "five W's and an H" questions.

To WHOM is the verse written?
WHAT is promised?
WHERE do we find grace?
WHEN do we receive it?
WHY was it given?
And HOW do we ask?

_____

_____

_____

_____

_____

_____

_____

_____

_____

_____

_____

_____

_____

_____

_____

_____

_____

PART 4

Secrets of Praise

There are some important and specific ways you can prevent those Sunday morning hassles. And it can begin on Saturday night.

1. Lay out clothes for the morning.
2. Set the table with cereal bowls and juice glasses. Set the timer on the coffee brewer *or* leave for church early and enjoy breakfast at a drive-thru.
3. Read several psalms of praise and worship before retiring. God can work on your heart, mind, and emotions through the night—just take a look at Psalm 16:7.
4. Go to bed a little earlier!
5. When you wake up Sunday morning, spend a quiet moment in prayerful preparation before you even get out of bed.

This evening just before bed, brew yourself a cup of tea, find a quiet corner and curl up with today's reading and your Bible. Take fifteen minutes to slowly meditate on these descriptions of Jesus, thanking Him for who He is . . . in your own words.

A Star . . . Numbers 24:17
Man of Sorrows . . . Isaiah 53:3
The Ancient of Days . . . Daniel 7:9
Servant . . . Matthew 12:18
The Holy One of God . . . Mark 1:24
Dayspring . . . Luke 1:78
Teacher . . . John 3:2
I Am . . . John 8:58
Rock . . . 1 Corinthians 10:4
The Indescribable Gift . . . 2 Corinthians 9:15
Chief Cornerstone . . . Ephesians 2:20
Our Hope . . . 1 Timothy 1:1.
The Man . . . 1 Timothy 2:5-6
Heir of All Things . . . Hebrews 1:2

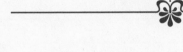

Let's be real. Do not-so-nice words trip off your tongue when your day goes haywire? For that matter, are there other quirky things you do when frustrated—slam your fist, hit a wall, or bang your steering wheel?

Take a look at Daniel 6:6-12 for a glimpse at a man whose first response always seemed to be the right response. When Daniel got wind of the awful decree, what was the very first thing he did? Notice verse 10 and the fact that Daniel prayed in full view of the town. What do you think was on his mind?

Make an exchange! Trade those not-so-nice words and actions for words of thanks and actions of obedience.

_____

_____

_____

_____

_____

_____

_____

_____

_____

_____

_____

_____

_____

_____

_____

Psalm 103 is a great psalm to use when you want to praise God for exactly who He is. Notice how the psalm begins and ends. Ask God right now to help you praise Him from your innermost being.

Next, personalize verses 2 through 5. Slowly and thoughtfully consider His benefits toward you—how He has forgiven your sins, healed you when you were sick, and lifted you when you were at your lowest.

Decide right now to keep Psalm 103 handy and ready for when Blue Monday, Wednesday, or Thursday comes along.

Have you ever seen a dry, barren desert suddenly spring to vibrant life after a rain shower? You wouldn't believe how drastic and miraculous the change can be. That's exactly how the Spirit of Christ can revive us out of a dry spell. Suddenly. Unexpectedly. Gloriously.

For a good word picture, read Isaiah 35:1-7. That portion of Scripture is talking about the return of the Lord Jesus, but the beautiful descriptions can also apply to you today.

For extra encouragment, underline verses 3 and 4!

Sometimes we demonstrate better responsibility for our attitude when we enlist the help of others. Ask a trusted friend to hold you accountable, to help you make the right choices. Ask your friend to nail you when he or she observes you handling a certain tough time with a complaining or grumbling spirit.

Feel uncomfortable with the idea? If so, remember this— Someone far greater than your friend is watching.

_____

_____

_____

_____

_____

_____

_____

_____

_____

_____

_____

_____

_____

_____

_____

_____

_____

_____

Take a look at 1 Peter 1:6-9. According to Peter, exactly why does God permit trials to come our way? Just how precious is your faith?

It will help you to know that Peter was writing to Christians who *really* were being tested by fire. They lived under the reign of the madman Nero and refused to worship him. As a result, believers had to face lions in the coliseum, not to mention everyday abuse and maltreatment. Theirs was a genuine test of faith. Yet history records that many of these early believers remained undaunted in their testimony. Their faith was neither scorched nor tarnished by complaints. They shined for God.

How can their gleaming example encourage you today?

Take a stroll down memory lane and pull out an old family photo album. Let your eyes linger over each snapshot of mom, dad, children, aunts, and cousins—hugging, smiling, and laughing. Reach back in your mind and recall the most meaningful times you've enjoyed with family—that picnic in the park, the family softball game, a special anniversary or memorable birthday party.

Feels nice, doesn't it?

Now—transfer some of those warm, family feelings to your relationship with your heavenly Father. Imagine for a moment His joy when He hears your praise. Think of how instant He is in responding to your cry.

While the smiles and laughter are still dancing in your mind, talk with Him now—straight from the heart.

Aren't you glad the Holy Spirit wraps words around your feelings—especially when you don't seem to have words to pray?

Sometimes it's helpful to borrow the Spirit-inspired words of someone from Scripture when you pray. I'm sure Solomon, who incidentally never seemed at a loss for words, would not mind loaning you his prayer recorded in 1 Kings 8:56-61. Personalize it and make it your prayer to God.

_____

Are you one of those "prepared people"?

Heartaches and hardships down here on earth have a way of preparing us to meet God when we arrive in heaven. When we meet Jesus face to face, our hardships will have given us at least a *tiny* taste of what He went through to purchase our redemption. We will appreciate Him so much more. After all, what proof could you bring of your love and faithfulness if this life left you totally unscarred? How could you appreciate at all the scarred hands with which Christ will greet you?

Get better prepared today by spending a few moments alone with Colossians 3:1-4.

Do you and I really appreciate the power behind those few precious words . . . in Jesus' name? Do we understand the broad and sweeping access we have before the Father?

When the Lord invited His followers to go to the Father in His name, He was talking about a brand new relationship between the believer and God. Previously, men and women approached God with caution and great fear through the priests. But since the resurrection of Jesus, all believers can talk to God personally . . . directly . . . any time we want!

To get a clearer idea of what it means to go to God "in Jesus' name," take a close look at Hebrews 10:19-23. Then tonight, as you lay your head on your pillow after your nightly prayer, take a moment to reflect on the marvelous access you enjoy before the Father.

The word picture Jesus used in John 7:38-39 is almost startling. What does the term *river* or *stream* imply about the outflow of the Spirit's life from within us? How would you describe the outflow from your life? A stream? A trickle? Take time with your Lord today to clear out any obstructions or rubbish that might be hindering the spring from "bubbling up" within you.

_____

John Donne said, "No man is an island, entire of itself; every man is a piece of the continent, a part of the main." It's good to be linked with other believers, isn't it? Think of the many benefits you've received from your fellowship with other Christians.

But don't forget—you benefit others as well. Take time to fill up on the advice of Romans 15:1-7. Will you commit yourself anew to pouring your love and counsel and prayers into a fellow believer trapped in the drain-and-fill cycle?

Take a look at your address book. There are probably big circles around the names of special people in your life. Now, take a glance at those names you've crossed out or erased. Have any idea where those people are or what they're doing?

Aren't you glad that God's Book of Life doesn't resemble your address book with all its splotched and smeared names? Want to know more about that Book of Life which includes your name? Turn to Revelation 20:11-15 and then praise God in your heart that He always uses permanent ink!

Have any doubt about that? For assurance, read Revelation 3:5.

"Count Your Blessings!" You've probably sung this old hymn (or heard it sung) scores of times. Whether at old-fashioned camp meetings or at Sunday evening services in a country church. Remember the tune? Maybe you haven't sung it for a while, but now is the time to sing it afresh. And remember . . . sing it with gusto. After all, you've got a lot of good gifts to thank God for!

When upon life's billows you are tempest tossed,
When you are discouraged, thinking all is lost,
Count your many blessings, name them one by one,
And it will surprise you what the Lord hath done.

Are you ever burdened with a load of care?
Does the cross seem heavy you are called to bear?
Count your many blessings, every doubt will fly,
And you will be singing as the days go by.

Count your blessings, name them one by one;
Count your blessings, see what God hath done;
Count your blessings, name them one by one;
Count your many blessings, see what God hath done.

Wouldn't you like praise to be a bigger part of your daily routine? I know I would. Let me give you an idea that has helped me to praise God . . . from my heart.

Try memorizing, if you haven't already, the Doxology:

Praise God from whom all blessings flow;
Praise Him all creatures here below;
Praise Him above, ye heavenly host;
Praise Father, Son, and Holy Ghost.

Now, say it! Sing it in the shower as you start your day. Think about it while you're waiting in line . . . at the fast-food drive-in, the bank window, or the grocery store check-out. Say it at the dinner table to replace your usual blessing for the food. Finally, whisper it as you feel yourself drifting off to sleep at night.

You think *your* circumstances are bad! Take a look at 2 Kings 25:1-12 at what God's people faced during the Babylonian invasion of Jerusalem. Now, picturing all that horror and confusion, read Jeremiah's assessment of those circumstances in Lamentations 3:21-25.

Did Jeremiah's faith rest on what he knew to be true about God, or on his own assessment of the cruel and horrible circumstances?

Can you pray Jeremiah's beautiful prayer in Lamentations 3 today as you consider your own circumstances, good or bad?

Here in southern California you'll hardly ever find newly-built homes made of brick. Know why? Because bricks crumble in earthquakes. That's another reason you won't find too many houses with basements. Most homes are built on concrete slab foundations so they will give more easily when the ground moves.

What kind of "home" are you building? Read Matthew 7:24-29 for a good master-building plan.

"I thank my God every time I remember you . . ." What kind of memories did Paul have of Philippi? Turn to Acts 16:11-15 for the beautiful story of Lydia. Read the verses and imagine the scene, picturing what went through Paul's mind. For another memory, skip down to Acts 16:25-40 and read about the amazing midnight conversion of an entire family.

Don't you think these beautiful memories—thrilling reminders of God's marvelous works—helped Paul in his loneliness? You bet!

Speaking of attitudes, the entire second chapter of Philippians reads like an attitude check-list. Verse 5 even says, "Your attitude should be the same as that of Christ Jesus."

Read verses 5 through 11 and take a check-up from the neck-up!

_____

_____
_____
_____
_____
_____
_____
_____
_____
_____
_____
_____
_____
_____
_____
_____
_____
_____
_____
_____
_____

If the season is right, clip a rosebud from a backyard bush. Or splurge and purchase an American Beauty bud from your florist. Place it in a vase near your desk or near your kitchen sink and watch it blossom from day to day. As its glory unfolds, take a moment to glory in one of Christ's amazing and lovely attributes.

It's great to think that God wants to do something new in our lives. But sometimes we feel tired of the way God works. We have a ho-hum "I've-seen-it-all-before" attitude. Read Isaiah 48:3-8 to see what God said to a bunch of Israelites who felt the same way. Learn from the Israelites' mistake. Start believing in the God who always tells us new things!

Chuck Swindoll urges believers to meditate on passages such as 1 Thessalonians 4:13-18—verses that describe the day when Jesus Christ will return to earth.

"Talk about high drama!" he writes. "Take a walk outside, weather permitting, with your New Testament in hand. Read again this startling glimpse into the future—*your* future. Let your eyes sweep the skies. Feel the thunder and joy and awe. Remind yourself that this experience could happen at any moment—even before you return from your walk . . . or draw your next breath."

Read Psalm 55:22, and then 1 Peter 5:7. Pour out your anxieties before Him today. He invites you to! You've nothing to lose but your fear.

Every puzzle piece of Scripture has a purpose. Some pieces are to make us "wise for salvation through faith in Christ Jesus." Other pieces are "useful for teaching, rebuking, correcting, and training in righteousness" (2 Timothy 3:15, 16).

In John 5:16-47, Jesus had a talk with some religious leaders who got hung up on a few of the puzzle pieces of Scripture. They were ignoring the frame. Take time to read those verses, zeroing in on verses 39-40, and see what Jesus has to say about the completed picture of the puzzle.

Mrs. Job may not have known how to handle her bad times because she didn't learn how to successfully deal with the good times. We take so much for granted— good health, full stomach, family safety, job security, sturdy roof over our heads.

How do we learn to respond well when life is good? It would help to remember that we must urgently seek God in the happy times as well as in the bad.

Read Habakkuk 3:17-18. Are you enjoying an abundant time of safety, good health, and happiness? You may not have sheep in a pen or cattle in the stalls, but list your favorite people and possessions and commit them to God right now.